Twitter In 30 Minutes

How to connect with interesting people, write great tweets, and find information that's relevant to you.

By Ian Lamont

Table Of Contents

Introduction

One January afternoon when I was at work, I saw a remarkable event unfold on Twitter.

It was around 3:30 p.m., and I was sitting at my computer. A few people I followed on Twitter suddenly began sending out short text messages (called "tweets") about a plane crash. The plane had apparently gone down in New York City, right in the Hudson River. New Yorkers in nearby buildings had seen the crash, or saw a plane in the river, and were sharing scraps of information in the short, 140-character text messages that Twitter allows.

I checked CNN and Google News. There were no official reports, but people on the ground were reporting a disaster. What was going on?

Then I saw someone share a remarkable photograph on Twitter:

The photo showed survivors standing on the wing, or stepping into a boat. The tweet that accompanied the photo said:

> There's a plane in the Hudson. I'm on the ferry going to pick up the people. Crazy.

I did not know Janis Krums, the person who took the photo or sent out that message on Twitter. But the information he posted on Twitter indicated that many passengers were alive, and were in the process of being rescued. Krums' friends shared the message, which was shared again to thousands of other people. Considering there was no official report or news account of what was happening, it was reassuring to see Krums' tweet.

The story of US Airways Flight 1549 is now well-known, thanks to the quick thinking and professionalism of Capt. Chesley B. "Sully" Sullenberger and his crew. More than 150 people were on the plane when it ran into a flock of geese and crash-landed. It could have been a tragedy. Yet every passenger survived.

But the crash-landing and rescue was important for another reason: It showed that Twitter was more than just a collection of fleeting observations about everyday life. Twitter could connect people to events, information and each other in ways that had never been experienced before.

What Is Twitter?

Twitter is a free tool that can connect you with interesting people, events and information. Twitter is available online at twitter.com, or as a free app that can be installed on a mobile phone or tablet. Millions of people all over the world consider Twitter to be as important to their daily communications routines as checking their email, sending text messages or catching up with friends on Facebook.

How do people use Twitter? I use it to keep up to date with current events, and to let people know about my business and whereabouts. Other people use it in different ways. Here are a few real examples:

- **Abby** (@AbbyLeighTaylor) is an Oklahoma native now living in Nashville. She loves using Twitter to connect with people who share her musical interests and Mexican food.

- **Fiona** (@EmeraldFaerie), a jewelry designer based in London, uses Twitter to show off her latest creations, and let customers know where they can be purchased.

- **The New York Public Library** (@nypl) tweets about 10 times per day about library programs, author appearances, photographs from its archives, and even job openings.

- **Steven** (@IamStevenT) is none other than Steven Tyler, the hardrock singer and TV personality. On Twitter, he talks about his tour schedule and television appearances, and also uses Twitter to connect with his fans.

- **Chayce** (@BehnkeChayce) is a young father and sports fanatic (Cleveland Browns, Buffalo Bills and Ohio State). He uses Twitter to talk about sports with other fans and ask questions related to his favorite teams.

- **Mark** (@mcuban) is a famous entrepreneur who uses Twitter to promote his business interests and basketball team, the Dallas Mavericks. He also answers questions from people who have seen him on TV, have read his book or follow his blog.

- **James** (@JamesBondTheDog) is the self-proclaimed "international hound dog of mystery." Like many parody accounts on Twitter, the focus is on humor ("Apple, you showed a squirrel at your press conference. You have my attention."). Many of James' followers are pet owners who have created Twitter accounts for their dogs.

As you can see from these examples, there are all kinds of people, organizations and interests represented on Twitter. Further, they use Twitter

3

for varied purposes — connecting with like-minded people, promoting their businesses or causes, and having fun.

However, if you are new to Twitter, it can be bewildering. There are strange symbols and unfamiliar conventions. It may not be apparent how Twitter can help you connect with people or start conversations.

This guide is intended to help you get your bearings and teach you how to get the most out of Twitter. *Twitter In 30 Minutes* concentrates on core skills and use cases that a beginner should understand. In the next 30 minutes, you'll learn how to do everything from setting up and personalizing your account online or using a mobile phone (Chapter 2), to finding interesting people and topics to follow (Chapter 3). There's a chapter that discusses how to tweet (Chapter 4). You'll even learn a few tricks, ranging from hashtags to retweeting (Chapter 5).

What Can Twitter Do For You?

At its heart, Twitter lets you do three things:

1. **Broadcast to the world what you are doing, what you are thinking and who you are with**. The broadcasts are short messages called "tweets" that contain no more than 140 characters of text. It's also possible to add a photograph or a link to a news story as well. While anyone can see these tweets, the messages are most likely to be noticed by people who "follow" you on Twitter (more about that later).

2. **Monitor what other people are saying and doing**. Millions of ordinary people — as well as companies, schools, sports teams, charities, politicians and superstars — broadcast their own messages to the world. You can choose to follow the accounts of people you like or who you think are interesting. When you follow someone, you will be able to see their recent tweets. Some may even follow you back, to see what you have to say!

3. **Learn about the world**. Because people all over the world use Twitter to describe what they are doing, how they are feeling and what they are seeing, Twitter is a window into events, opinions, and

information. Want to know what other people think about the latest episode of your favorite TV show or sports team? Want to see photographs taken at a concert, beach or political rally? Twitter can let you do that. The flow of information is sometimes rough, but it grants an unfiltered view of the world, often before "official" sources of news weigh in.

We only have 30 minutes, so let's get started with Twitter!

CHAPTER ONE

A Brief Tour Of Twitter

Before I show you how to sign up for Twitter and start using the service, let's take a brief tour of Twitter to better understand how people use the service. We'll start with a famous person (Oprah Winfrey), move onto a Twitter account operated by a local business, and then see how several ordinary people use Twitter.

@Oprah

If you are sitting near a computer, or have a mobile phone, open a Web browser and type this into the address bar:

twitter.com/oprah

This is the Web address for Oprah Winfrey, the talented American television host, actress and media mogul. If you are sitting at a desktop computer, this is what you will see:

There's a lot going on. There are photos and videos on the left side of the page. Elsewhere there are multiple   references to tweets, followers, and "following," along with numbers. There are buttons and strange symbols.

There's even a square photo showing Oprah with a giant Afro hairstyle. What's happening here?

Think of twitter.com/oprah as Oprah's public display case. She (and her staff) determine nearly everything seen on this page. Most of the action takes place in the center of the screen. At the top of the page, you can see Oprah's name and her Twitter name, or "handle" — @Oprah (pronounced "at-Oprah"). Oprah has also included a photo of herself from the cover of her magazine. The Afro looks funny, but Oprah has a sense of humor and that's what she wants people to see!

Below this are some numbers corresponding to tweets, following, and followers. Here's what the numbers mean:

- **Tweets**: A tweet is a message that is no more than 140 characters in length. Oprah has sent out more than 7,000 such messages. This seems like a lot. However, she has been using Twitter for years. Considering each message takes anywhere between a few seconds and a minute to compose, it's not hard to create a thousand or more tweets in a single year. Oprah's most recent tweets are shown at the top of the page. If you keep scrolling down, Oprah's older tweets will be revealed.

- **Following**: This number refers to other Twitter accounts that Oprah follows. There are relatively few people on the list. If you click on the number, you will see that most of the people are media personalities, guests who have appeared on her show and her staff. But whenever one of them tweets something, Oprah will see it when she visits.

- **Followers**: Oprah has lots of fans, and a lot of them have chosen to "follow" Oprah. This means they will see Oprah's tweets when they look at Twitter, along with any other accounts they are following. Following a Twitter account is kind of like "friending" someone on Facebook, except it's only one-way. In other words, you can follow someone on Twitter, but unlike Facebook, you don't have to follow them back. In Oprah's case, millions of people are following her, but she doesn't have to reciprocate.

Below this section are Oprah's tweets. The tweets that Oprah and millions of other people create are really at the heart of Twitter. On Oprah's Twitter page, you will see a list of her most recent tweets. What is she talking about? Let's take a look:

The first thing to note is Oprah has a dialogue with her fans, the people she follows, and the people she supports. "@BishopJakes" and "@GaOWNers" are the Twitter accounts belonging to a person (Bishop TD Jakes in Dallas, Texas) or an organization (a Georgia fan club for the Oprah Winfrey Network). In the case of @BishopJakes, she is mentioning him because she wants to show support for his activities, which include programming on her TV network. For @GaOWNers, Oprah is responding to a technical question.

It may seem jarring to see these tiny fragments of unrelated conversations on someone's Twitter profile. That's just the nature of Twitter. Later, we'll learn how to expand these conversations and even join them.

Second, Oprah uses Twitter to promote her entertainment empire, as well as people and ideas she supports. Because she has so many followers on Twitter, mentioning or endorsing something is an extremely powerful promotional tool. Sometimes these products or ideas are associated with "hashtags," which are a word or phrase attached to a pound symbol. In

Chapter 3, we will learn more about hashtags.

Oprah is an unusual case, though. She was famous before she joined Twitter, which explains her 20 million-strong army of followers. This is rare. Very few people and organizations have this level of influence on Twitter. It's far more common to have just a few hundred followers. As you might expect, having a few hundred followers vs. millions of followers changes the nature of the discussions and interactions on Twitter.

@Momogoose

For our second example, we're going to look at a local business. Momogoose operates food trucks and small cafes in Boston and Cambridge, Massachusetts. I discovered one of their food trucks when I was a grad student, and was surprised to see the truck had a Twitter name — @momogoose — painted on the side, near the menu. What could a food truck possibly have to say on Twitter?

A lot, it turns out. Here's twitter.com/momogoose:

Like Oprah, Momogoose uses Twitter for promotional purposes and reaching out to fans. But the scale is much smaller. Momogoose's food trucks have only a few thousand followers, most of them are in the Boston area. Why do these people follow a food truck on Twitter? Obviously, they like the truck and its food, and following @momogoose on Twitter is a way of showing support. But it's also a way of finding out about Momogoose, the business.

Indeed, @momogoose sends out a regular stream of tweets on weekdays describing new dishes or specials. Based on these tweets, some followers may decide to visit the food truck for lunch from time to time. Even if the result is only two or three additional sales per day, that adds up over time. For Momogoose, Twitter is a free promotional tool that can help attract customers and generate revenue.

Momogoose also uses Twitter to connect with customers and other businesses in other ways. Some Twitter users ask questions, while others give feedback. @Momogoose is only too happy to engage with its customers using Twitter. Momogoose also follows many of its fans, as well as other local businesses.

@RobertFischer

Robert Fischer may not be a celebrity, but he is a very active person on Twitter, with more than 25,000 tweets. Here is his profile, located at twitter.com/RobertFischer:

As you can see from the @RobertFischer profile, Robert puts his interests front and center for other people to see. This helps potential followers decide whether or not to follow him.

The topics @RobertFischer tweets about run the gamut from bluegrass to programming to politics. Every now and then, he'll throw out a link to a funny video. He is very engaged with the people he follows and who follow him — he frequently responds to questions or comments on Twitter, and also uses it to ask questions related to software development.

@Jus_Tish

Like @RobertFisher, @Jus_Tish is a normal person (as opposed to a celebrity) using Twitter to talk about her interests and reach out to friends. Here's her profile page at twitter.com/jus_tish:

One thing that's worth noting: The identity of @Jus_Tish is not clear. She chose to use a nickname for her Twitter handle, and does not reveal any information about her hometown or occupation in her profile. While Twitter asks all new users to enter a full name when they register, you can also use nicknames, initials and fanciful identities. Anonymous or semi-anonymous Twitter identities give people more flexibility in terms of what they say and how they present themselves.

What does @Jus_Tish tweet about? She loves going to church. She likes music — about half of her tweets relate to something she's listening to or watching on YouTube. She actively participates in discussions about one of her favorite singers, Calvin Richardson (@ThePrinceOfSoul). She likes Chinese food, and sometimes talks about what she is watching on TV. @Jus_Tish also reaches out to a small circle of Twitter connections to offer reassurance, updates or observations about life. Her tweets are sprinkled with great quotes.

@Jus_Tish also tweets a lot. In a typical day, Tish sends dozens of tweets, especially in the evening. How can she do it? She has an iPhone, and uses the Twitter app for the iPhone, which allows her to tweet from practically anywhere.

@Caliguy16

There is one last Twitter account I want to use as an example. Here's the account for @caliguy16:

As you start to use Twitter, you will see many accounts that have an image of an egg instead of a person or logo. Why the egg? If someone starts an account but doesn't provide a profile picture, then Twitter will default to a graphic of an egg on a colored background. The different colors don't mean anything, but the egg is associated with "newbie" accounts, belonging to people who just got started with Twitter or those who abandoned the accounts not long after registering them. Indeed, @caliguy16 tweeted twice (in 2008) and then abandoned Twitter.

The reasons aren't clear why @caliguy16 gave up. If I were to hazard a guess, I would point to the lack of network. He never followed anyone and was followed by only one person — a local politician who barely used Twitter himself. Because @caliguy16 did not follow anyone, this means there would have been no information or people to talk with in his timeline. If you don't build your network, Twitter will seem like a boring place.

I also want to mention something about the egg icon. While there's nothing wrong with being a newbie on Twitter, there's no excuse for being represented by an egg. Egg profiles send negative signals to other people on Twitter, who may avoid following accounts that don't appear very dedicated to the Twitter community.

Fortunately, it's easy enough to create and upload a profile picture using your phone or Twitter.com on a PC. I'll show you how to do this in the next chapter.

CHAPTER TWO

Signing Up For Twitter

There are two ways to sign up for Twitter: Online (using a Web browser on your PC or laptop), or on a mobile device (such as a phone or tablet). Both ways are easy, but I recommend doing it online because you are less likely to make a typing mistake (important for usernames and passwords).

How To Register Online

Open up your Web browser, and type twitter.com into the address bar. You should see something like this:

To create a Twitter account, you only need to submit a valid email address and password. The email address is required to confirm the account, and is also used to send you notifications and other messages (later on you can select the messages you want to receive from Twitter). You can leave the name field blank, but later you will have to add something, even if it's a fake name, a nickname, or initials.

Here's the next screen:

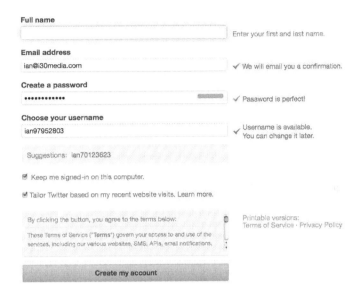

There are a few fields worth noting:

Name: If you left it blank on the first screen, you will have to fill it out here. You don't have to use your real name, and you can change it later. For the sake of this example, I will put in my initials, "IL", before pressing the continue button.

Username: This string of letters and numbers will become the Twitter handle. But there's a problem — Twitter "has suggested I choose ian97952803 as a username. I don't want to have @ian97952803 as my Twitter handle, as it's too long and too hard to remember. Twitter also suggests ian70132623, which is equally bad. I want something that is more personal or relates to my company. The username "ian" is already taken, but the username "author_ian" is available. So my Twitter handle will be @author_ian.

Some people like to use Twitter usernames that are similar to their real names. For instance, the singer Alicia Keys uses @aliciakeys while Bob Dylan has @bobdylan. My personal Twitter account, which I have used since 2007, is @ilamont. Handles like this are easy to remember, but some people don't want to directly connect their identities to Twitter. Another issue: It's harder to choose handles based on common names, because other people may have already chosen them.

Twitter allows people to change their usernames, but I advise to pick one that you like now and stick with it.

Keep me signed in: If this is a computer that only you use, keep this box checked. If it's the family computer, or a public computer at a library or school, keep it blank, or anyone else who has access to the browser may be able to post tweets on your account. This can be embarrassing or even cause real trouble.

Tailor Twitter based on my recent website visits: Checking this box lets Twitter monitor many of the sites that you visit, and "tailor" advertisements and other content based on what you've viewed on other websites. Imagine what sorts of assumptions Twitter will make based on the sites your 7-year-old son checks out, or the fact that you once looked the Home Depot website to see what time the nearest branch closes. Twitter may assume you must love Legos and riding mowers, and mercilessly bombard you with such ads. My advice: Leave this box unchecked.

Once you have made your choices, click the "Create My Account" button. You will be brought to a quick tutorial that explains what tweets are and why you should follow people.

Twitter wants you to start following people right away, and asks you to follow five accounts from a list of recommended accounts. If you are a teenager, you might find the suggestions appealing — the list is dominated by the latest pop stars. But scrolling down, I find the accounts from a few people I can grudgingly follow, including @Oprah:

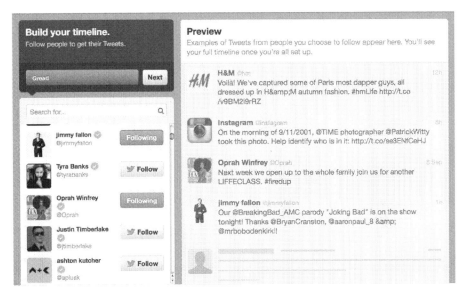

You'll then be prompted to follow even more people from category-based lists. There are celebrities, but Twitter also presents other categories, such as people in technology, politics, fashion, health, religion as well as charitable organizations and news services. Follow @RedCross, @Smithsonian, @NYTimes, @DalaiLama, @Pontifex (the Twitter handle for Pope Francis), and any other accounts that strike your fancy. Twitter's recommendations are all "famous" accounts with lots of followers. You'll have a chance to follow ordinary folks later.

Importing Email Address Books Into Twitter

The next screen requires some care to navigate. Twitter will help you find friends to follow by matching other people's Twitter accounts with the email addresses in your Yahoo, Gmail, Hotmail or address book. It's a very good way to find friends and colleagues with Twitter accounts, even if they are using an obscure Twitter handle. For instance, a few dozen people showed up in the left column when I let Twitter sync to my Yahoo account:

The suggestions are useful. However, there are some great dangers associated with letting Twitter gather all the email addresses in your address book. For instance, did you notice the link that says "Invite 282 to join Twitter"? If I click that link, Twitter will spam nearly 300 of my other Yahoo friends who are not on Twitter. No thanks! In addition, there are no guarantees that Twitter won't abuse the emails I send them, or lose control of the data if someone hacks Twitter's database.

Based on these facts, I do not recommend syncing your address books to Twitter. Instead, click the barely noticeable "Skip" link near the bottom of the left column.

Customizing Your Twitter Profile Online

You'll be brought to the screen that lets you customize your profile:

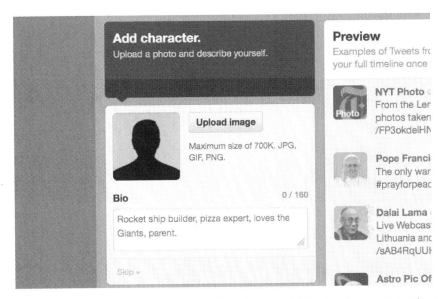

Take a little time to add a photo and fill out a short bio. It takes just a minute or two.

Click the Upload button to find a photo on your hard drive. Most people use recent headshots, but photos from childhood or pets are common. You can change the photo at any time.

The bio has to be less than 140 characters. You may want to use funny descriptors ("Sharp-dressed taco aficionado and die-hard Eagles fan") or something more down-to-earth ("Real estate lawyer serving greater Phoenix"). I chose something in between, with a cute picture of myself at age 4:

Confirming Your Twitter Account Registration

Once you're done, you'll be prompted to confirm your Twitter account. Go to the email account you used to register for Twitter, and look for the email from Twitter that says "Confirm your account now".

Press the button or the link. Your account will be confirmed! You are ready to start following other people (Chapter 3) and tweeting (Chapter 4).

How To Register Using A Phone Or Tablet

Registering on a mobile device, such as a mobile phone or tablet, is quick. Twitter makes apps for most platforms, including:

- **Android**: Phones and tablets from Samsung, LG, Nexus, and many others.

- **iOS**: iPhone, iPad, iPod touch

- **BlackBerry**

- **Windows Phone**

- **Some older handsets**

In this section, I'll cover Android and iOS devices, which dominate the market. The Twitter app can be downloaded via Apple's App Store and Google Play. Setup processes are nearly identical. If you have a Windows Phone, BlackBerry, or other device, go to twitter.com/download to get the app.

Download the Twitter app from the app store. The first time you open it, you will be asked if you want to let Twitter access location data. This basically means Twitter wants to know where you are. This data might be appended to tweets and photos you distribute. If you are sensitive about privacy and tracking, do not accept this option.

iOS devices (such as the iPhone and iPad) will also ask you if you want to turn on push notifications. It's a good way to stay active with Twitter as you get started, but over time, be prepared to get lots of notifications of people following you or mentioning you in a tweet.

Opening the app for the first time, you will see an attractive splash screen and buttons to sign up or sign in. Press the Sign Up button. The first registration screen will look something like this, depending on the type of device (phone or tablet) and operating system (Android or iOS):

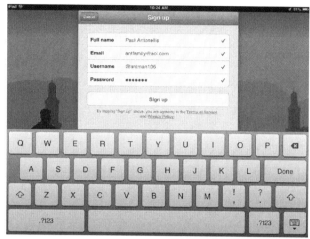

The fields on the Twitter registration screen may already be filled in, based on the Gmail or Apple ID credentials you used when you first set up the device. If not, enter a name, email address and Twitter username, which will be your handle on Twitter. The app will warn you if you select a username that has already been registered by someone else.

The app will ask if it can access the contact list on your phone. Agreeing to this will let Twitter match the email addresses in your contact list with existing Twitter accounts. The image below shows the prompt on an iPad on the left, while the image on the right shows the matches I found in my own Gmail address book on an Android phone:

22

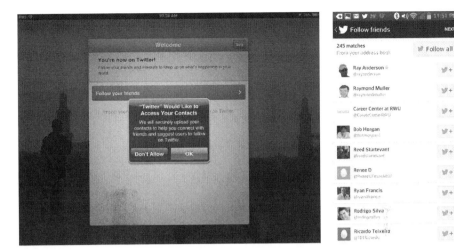

You can follow everyone at once by tapping the Follow All button, or individually follow people by clicking on the bird icon with the plus symbol. I recommend the latter option, as there may be some Twitter accounts that belong to old contacts whom you do not want to follow.

Importing Phone Contacts Into Twitter

Once you have made your selections, tap the Next button. Twitter will prompt you to invite all of the other contacts in your address book to Twitter. Do not check off any names or the Select All button. Doing so will send a wave of spam to everyone else you know. Most of the people will not be interested in Twitter, and and may not be pleased by the spam from you.

Instead, click Next. You will be brought to Twitter's "Suggestions", which consists mostly of celebrities. You can follow the people listed by tapping the bird icon, or click the link at the bottom to browse more categories, such as Art, Books, Funny and Sports. Once you are finished, click Done.

At this point, you will be brought to the home screen of the Twitter app. This displays a timeline consisting of tweets of the accounts you follow. You can also start tweeting by tapping the icon in the upper right corner that looks like a square with a fountain pen (this is also covered in Chapter 4).

Customizing Your Profile On A Mobile Device

But there's one more important thing to do: Finish your profile. To do so, tap the icon that looks like the silhouette of a person. On the left, we see Janet editing her profile on an Android phone. On the right, Paul edits his profile on an iPad:

If you're following along on your own mobile device, you may wonder why there is a picture of an egg for each of these profiles. The answer: You haven't set a profile photo yet. Do this now. Tap the photo, and a small pop-up window will offer you the option to edit your profile. Here are the elements that you can change:

- **Photo**: Tap the photo (or egg) to take a new profile photo with the camera, or select an existing photo on your phone or tablet.

- **Header**: This is an optional background image that appears on your Twitter profile. I don't recommend using this, as it usually clashes with the profile photo.

- **Name**: You can change your name. If you prefer to be anonymous or semi-anonymous, use your first name or something fanciful.

- **Location**: Most people give the nearest city or region. You can leave this field blank if you want.

- **Website**: If you have a website, enter the address here. Some people use the address of a blog, or their company's website address. Others type in links to their Facebook or Instagram pages.

- **Bio**: You only have 140 characters, which is less than 15 words for most people. People on Twitter tend to be casual with their bios, but you can also be formal if you have a professional image to project. Make each word count!

CHAPTER THREE

Following People And Organizations On Twitter

Now that you have activated your Twitter account, you can start tweeting right away (this is explained in more detail in the next chapter). However, I suggest following more people before you start tweeting. There are several reasons for this:

- The more people you follow, the more likely you are to see interesting things that you can share, explore or respond to
- Some people you follow on Twitter will follow you back, which can help build your Twitter network and increase the likelihood of your tweets being seen and responded to.

How To Follow Someone On Twitter

So you've signed up for Twitter, reserved your Twitter handle, set up a profile, and are ready to seize Twitter by the beak. This requires tweeting (described in Chapter 4), but you also want to see what other people are tweeting about and sharing on Twitter. To see other people's tweets, you'll need to start following people. If you don't, Twitter will seem empty and boring, and you will quickly lose interest.

As described in the previous chapter, Twitter encourages people to follow celebrity accounts when they sign up to use the service. Twitter also urges users to upload their contact lists, and will try to match the email addresses of your friends and contacts with existing Twitter accounts.

But what if you want to follow a Twitter account after you have registered? Here's how:

Following An Account Online

Once you are registered for Twitter and have logged in, go to the Twitter profile and click the Follow button. Below is an example of @GovChristie, the Twitter page of Governor Chris Christie of New Jersey. You can visit it by typing twitter.com/ChrisChristie into the address bar of your browser. The follow button is located below the description:

If you click the Follow button, all the recent tweets created by @GovChristie will start showing up in your timeline. Your timeline consists of tweets from the Twitter accounts that you follow. The more accounts you follow, the more tweets you will see in your feed.

Following Someone On Your Phone Or Tablet

Open the Twitter app. At the top of the screen, you will see an icon that looks like a magnifying glass. Tap it to open the search feature. In the field provided, type the account name of the person or organization you want to follow, including the @ symbol:

Tap the "Go to" Twitter handle. The profile of the account will open up at the top of the screen. Tap the Follow button.

Protected Accounts

A small number of Twitter accounts are closed off to public viewing. The tweets are "protected" and it's impossible to see who the owner is following or is followed by, unless he or she lets you follow the account. Here's an example:

Why would someone set up a protected Twitter account, or switch his or her account from open to protected? Here are some reasons:

- The owner does not want his or her tweets to be public for personal reasons, or a desire for privacy.

- Certain people want to temporarily avoid scrutiny for a brief period of time, such as a celebrity embroiled in a scandal. He or she will re-open the account once the hubbub dies down.

- People or organizations want to reserve a Twitter handle so no one else grabs it, but the owner is not ready to start tweeting.

- Businesses want to close their feed to everyone except confirmed customers.

Note that it is possible to follow a protected account. However, you will need to be approved by the owner first. Simply click the Follow button, and a notification will be sent to the owner. He or she can then approve or reject the request. If you are approved, you will be able to see his or her tweets.

If you get rejected, don't take it so hard. There are many other interesting accounts to follow, as we'll see later this chapter.

How To Unfollow Twitter Accounts

Here's the situation: You're following @Oprah, but the relentless promotion of her media empire on Twitter is driving you nuts. It's gotten to the point that when Oprah's profile picture pops up in your Twitter feed, you involuntarily groan in anticipation of another self-congratulatory tweet about a free car giveaway, her latest movie or her shows on OWN. Please, make it stop!

The easy way to unfollow @Oprah, or anyone else, is to simply click the Unfollow button on their Twitter profile. To ditch Oprah on Twitter, you would go to @Oprah's online Twitter profile (twitter.com/oprah). The blue button confirms you are following her, but if you hover your mouse over the button, it turns to a red Unfollow button:

Once that happens, @Oprah's tweets will no longer be automatically fed into your Twitter feed. Huzzah!

How To Unfollow Lots Of People Quickly

If you want to unfollow lots of people at once, there is an easy way to do it.

Go to your own profile and select Following. Doing so brings up a list of all of the Twitter accounts you are following. Hover over one of the buttons, and it turns to a red Unfollow button:

On the mobile app, there will be blue buttons with a bird logo and a check mark. Press the button next to each account you want to unfollow.

How Many Accounts Should I Follow?

How many people and organizations should you follow on Twitter? That's up to you. I have seen people who follow tens of thousands of other Twitter accounts. While they never have a shortage of tweets to read, I question the value of the information they are getting — the most interesting or relevant tweets tend to be lost in the firehose.

A better strategy, at least in the beginning, is to follow a limited number of people or organizations that are more likely to maintain your interest and engage with you. Once you've gotten the hang of Twitter, grow the list as slowly or as quickly as you like.

Following 50 other Twitter accounts is a good starting point. It doesn't take that long to follow 50 accounts, and if you pick wisely, you'll start getting value from your list right away. Tips on how to pick are included below.

Who Should I Follow?

Twitter has mechanisms to help you find people to follow. If you've registered for Twitter (Chapter 2), you've already seen how Twitter suggests celebrities and can leverage your email contacts list to identify friends and coworkers on Twitter. But how can you identify other accounts to follow?

For a rewarding Twitter experience, it's crucial to identify accounts that are close to your own connections and interests. They might be friends, family members or colleagues. They could be people living in your town or city, or people from a location that's close to your heart — the place where you grew up, a favorite vacation spot, or a city or country you would like to visit.

I also advise new Twitter users to follow people who have shared interests as well as specialty accounts devoted to a cause or hobby. Identify the experts or people with the best insights, as well as sources of information that lead the conversation, such as a well-known publication or thought leader.

For instance, do you like political news? Are you the kind of person who feels a tingle of excitement when there's a scandal brewing, or do you like to follow wonky policy debates? Then follow @politico, which is the Twitter account for the popular Washington-based news site of the same name. Political junkies may also want to follow the accounts of certain reporters, pundits and politicians.

Or maybe you are a knitting fanatic. If that's the case, then @KnittingDaily is a good account to follow. People in this community share tips and new designs. There are even indie knitting rebels at @YarnHarlot and author/"knitting detective" @catbordhi:

Basketball freaks have their own buzz going on Twitter. This is due in large part to the active participation by professional and college players...and their fans. I recommend @SLAMonline or @ESPNNBA, as well as the account of Detroit Piston Charlie Villanueva (@CV31).

There is a totally different culture around disabilities. People with spinal cord injuries, blind users and patients with more obscure health conditions share their views of the world, and the advocacy efforts promoted by the disability rights community. In addition, family members, advocates and organizations join the discussions. The accounts operated by Paralympic gold medallist @JessicaLong and @AAPD are good places to start.

At the start of this guide, I showed the account of @JamesBondTheDog. What if you're a cat person? Twitter has you covered! One of the most popular Twitter cats is @sockington ("I am Jason Scott's cat"), with more than 1.7 million followers on Twitter. And then there's @RealGrumpyCat:

You get the idea. Practically every interest, hobby, cause, and condition is represented on Twitter. Sometimes it takes a little digging to find relevant and interesting accounts (more on that in the next section), but once you follow them, you will feel like you've connected with a group of kindred souls (or cats).

How Do I Find Certain Accounts To Follow?

So you have an idea of who you want to follow. The next step is actually locating them on Twitter. It's not as easy as it sounds. While some people have obvious account names (such as @Oprah) others choose unusual Twitter handles. For instance, Ashton Kutcher uses @aplusk. Many non-celebrities also use handles that are based on their names, but if people have same or similar names it may not be clear which person to follow.

There are ways of cutting through the confusion, however.

How To Find Friends On Twitter

Twitter is used by hundreds of millions of people, so there is a good chance that at least a few people you know have active Twitter accounts. You may have discovered a few when you registered your account, if you used the option that lets Twitter scan your contact lists.

There are other ways to find friends on Twitter. The easiest way to do it is to ask…on Facebook! Here's the type of message to post:

> "Friends, I am building up my Twitter network at @bobsmith102. Please follow me or your leave your Twitter handle in the comments to this Facebook post."

Another method: Search your email for people who have used their Twitter handles in an email signature. Searching for "Twitter" in Gmail, Yahoo Mail or AOL usually turns up a few results.

You can also Google people's Twitter handles. Just type their name and "twitter" and see what turns up. Note that this method will not identify people who have used a real name when they registered for Twitter. In addition, there is a good chance that other people with similar names will turn up in the results.

How To Find Local Accounts To Follow

The great thing about tapping into local accounts in Twitter is it allows you to gain new insights into your community and the people who live there.

The easiest starting points:

Local newspapers and reporters: You may already get the local paper delivered to your house. However, I have found that Twitter accounts operated by newspapers sometimes have extra goodies, including live reports from local events or details that get left out of the print edition.

To start following the account, look at the print or online edition of the paper. The front page will often have a little blurb that says "Follow us on Twitter!", with either a link to the Twitter profile or the account name preceded by an

@ symbol. For instance, my local paper's Twitter account is @NewtonTab. To go to the Twitter profile, I just type "twitter.com", a forward slash, and "newtontab" in the address bar of the browser, without any spaces:

What to expect? Besides links to online news stories or breaking police and fire incidents, additional information gets shared. Here's one update from my local paper, talking about a local Little League team:

The reporter who wrote it let his followers know that the game can be watched on NESN, a sports cable channel serving New England. This is information I can use!

Besides following the account of the paper or individual reporters, you can also use these accounts to find other local people or institutions to follow. For instance, my local paper often shares messages from our mayor, Setti Warren:

Clicking his Twitter name brings up his profile:

From there, all I need to do is press the Follow button, and I'll be able to see the mayor's tweets in my timeline.

Local bloggers: Somewhere in your community, someone is writing a blog. Blog authors are people who feel compelled to write about something. It could be about their lives, their hobbies or interests, their children, their areas of expertise, or even uncomfortable topics such as living with disease or divorce.

You may not know who these people are. Indeed, they may not want you to know who they are, but they are there, and they love to write. Oftentimes, they love to tweet, too.

To find local bloggers who write about local issues, Google the name of your town or community and the word "blog". Check out the blogs that are highlighted, and look for a Twitter symbol on the front page. Click the symbol to be taken to the blogger's Twitter account.

Local businesses and organizations: In Chapter 1, I used the example of the @momogoose food truck, which uses Twitter to stay connected with its customers. This is not unusual. The next time you visit local coffee shop, clothes boutique, restaurant or library, look around for a "Follow us on Twitter!" sign. These days, savvy businesses use Twitter to connect with local patrons who want to learn about incoming products, special deals, new branches or other insights.

You don't need to visit the building in person to find out if a business has a Twitter account. Google the company online, and see if the company's website contains a link to a Twitter account.

Random local people: Once you've identified local media, bloggers and businesses, and are following them on Twitter, check out the "Following" and "Followers" links on their profile pages. You're sure to find local people in the lists. For instance, in my local newspaper's Followers list, I found these Twitter accounts:

Clicking through to the profiles, I was able to identify people in my community. How? Sometimes people include their hometowns on their Twitter profiles, or they may reference people, places, or issues in their tweets, which indicate where they are located.

You can do the same thing, starting with local media and businesses and trying to identify local followers. You may not know these people, and they may not give their real names. Nevertheless, it's OK to follow them. They may even follow you back!

Accounts To Avoid

Before I follow anyone in Twitter, I check their tweets. If they don't tweet often, or the tweets are boring (for instance, just links to news stories) I won't follow them. Here are some other red flags:

Egg accounts. Egg accounts are often new or abandoned accounts, created by people who don't know how to set a profile picture. For people who have just started tweeting, having an egg account is normal (maybe you're an egg, too!). However, egg accounts that haven't been updated in months or years are not worth following. The people who own them have given up on Twitter, and most likely won't ever share something of interest.

Rude birds. Some people on Twitter use Twitter to belittle others or share intimate details of their warped lives or bizarre thoughts. The tweets are littered with swears and stupidity. Sometimes the accounts belong to teens who don't know any better. Sometimes they belong to adults who haven't matured. Rarely do they offer insights or information of value. Don't bother following them.

Spam accounts. Not long after you start using Twitter, you will receive a notification that someone is following you. Most of the time, the followers are legit — maybe they are people you know, or people who are following you because of some shared interest.

But others may look a little...off. The tweets seem vapid or otherwise inauthentic. They follow hundreds or thousands of people, but have very few people following them back. Links appear in their feeds that don't come from well-known domains. In addition, the profile pictures tend to show unusually attractive people. Here's an example, showing the profile on the left and the tweets on the right:

Don't get your hopes up if you discover someone like this following you. Random, attractive people probably don't want to follow you (or me, for that matter!). In fact, such accounts do not belong to attractive people tweeting about football, travel, and hooking up. These accounts actually belong to spammers, and my guess is most of them are unattractive, basement-dwelling losers who are tweeting links to low-grade dating sites, advertisements or online shopping portals that might generate a few pennies every time someone clicks. Don't click the links, and don't follow them back.

Help! I'm Being Followed

What happens when a normal person or account follows you? This is the message that you will see in your inbox:

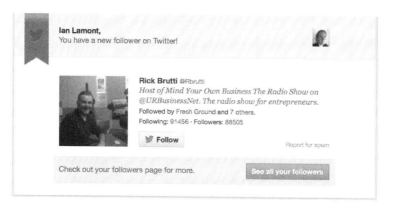

You can also see a list of your followers, presented in reverse-chronological order. Go to your profile page on Twitter and click the Followers link:

It may seem strange that these people are following your tweets. Who are they? How did they find out about you? What are their intentions?

For most accounts, it's easy to figure out who they are: Just click on the link to see their profile page and the recent tweets they've made.

As for how they found out about you, and why they are following you, those are harder questions to answer. In many cases, they may have stumbled upon you by using Twitter search or looking at someone else's list of followers (for instance, if you follow @Oprah or the local newspaper, you will show up on those two accounts' lists of followers). They may think your tweets are funny or insightful, or you share some common interest.

Most of the time, it's harmless attention. These strangers will see your tweets, and may even start a dialogue at some point. But "following" is not synonymous with "stalking." Twitter creates value by sharing information and letting people and organizations expand their networks, even with strangers who they may never meet in person.

Remember also that anyone can see your tweets. All they need to do is load your profile into their web browsers. Even if they aren't following you, they will still see your tweets.

In other words, your tweets are public information. If you don't want anyone to see them, then you should protect your tweets…or not use Twitter at all.

Information on how to block specific users from following you and how to protect your tweets is included at the end of this chapter.

Recommended Accounts

If you are using Twitter on the Web, you'll notice a list of recommended accounts when you go to your home page at twitter.com. They are listed under "Who To Follow":

The accounts that appear there are not random. The top-listed account is often a "Promoted" account, which means that someone is paying for it to show up there. As for the other accounts displayed under Who To Follow, Twitter uses algorithms and behavioral data to generate the recommendations. Sometimes the recommended accounts are relevant, but I've noticed celebrities tend to be shown to new users. If you are the kind of person who likes TMZ and *People* magazine, having celebrity tweets show up in your timeline is probably a dream come true. But for the rest of us, it quickly gets old.

There are other reasons not to follow celebrities. I've found that many of them tend to be in promotion mode most of the time, and are highly unlikely to start a dialogue with individual fans. It's not because they are jerks. They simply don't have the time. For instance, even if @Oprah took a break from promoting the latest Oprah Book Club selection and decided to say "Hi!" to each one of her Twitter followers every minute of every day, it would take approximately 14,000 years to get through the more than 20,000,000 accounts currently following her.

My recommendation is to avoid most of the recommended accounts, and instead follow friends' Twitter accounts, local accounts and shared interest accounts using the methods described earlier. You can also use Twitter search, described below.

Twitter Search And Hashtags

Twitter's Search feature is a useful way to find accounts to follow. On Twitter.com, the search window is located at the top of the page. Just start typing in names, and people's accounts will begin to show up:

This is a great way to find accounts of people you know or have heard about. I've been able to track down the Twitter accounts of musicians, business people, authors and old friends in this manner. However, there are some limitations to searching for names:

- Some people use Twitter without revealing their real names in their profiles. If you search for their names, you won't be able to find them.

- People with common names can be difficult to find on Twitter.

Here's an example that helps illustrate the problem. Let's say I wanted to find Bill Lee, the quirky Red Sox pitching ace from the 1970s dubbed "Spaceman". Typing "Bill Lee" into Twitter Search brings back a list of other men and women named Bill Lee, William Lee or Billie Lee, but not my childhood baseball hero. However, by changing the search terms to Spaceman Bill Lee, he shows up:

The other way to use Twitter search to find accounts is to use words or phrases that people might use in a tweet. For instance, if you wanted to find other people who like Oprah's Book Club, searching for that phrase brings up some interesting results, ranging from discussions of specific books to jokes:

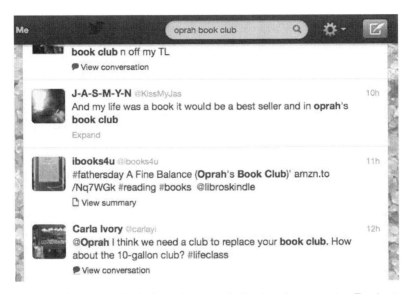

You can use the same technique to search for local accounts. For instance, if you like Chicago basketball, search for "Chicago Bulls". If you are interested in politics in San Diego, search for "San Diego politics".

Hashtags: What They Do, And How To Use Them

You may notice that some words in tweets have the hashtag symbol (#) added to the front. Occasionally, there will be a hashtagged phrase or acronym with all of the spaces and periods removed. Hashtags are a Twitter convention that lets people easily find tweets about the same topic. By adding a hashtag to the front of a word or phrase, it turns it into link that is hooked up to Twitter's search engine. Click the link, and the most recent tweets that include the same hashtag are displayed. Here's what shows up when I click on #Bulls:

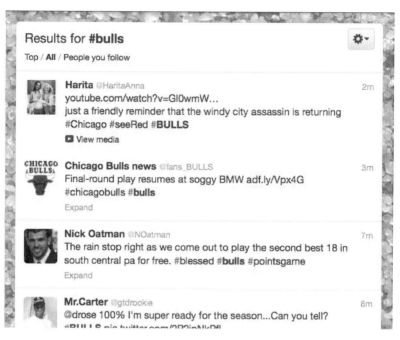

Hashtags serve other useful functions as well. They alert other Twitter followers to the fact that the tweet is about a certain topic that may otherwise not be apparent. Let's say you're watching the Oscars on TV, and you see someone wearing a beautiful dress glide by the camera. You could ask your Twitter followers:

Many people may not know what you are talking about. But they will if you add an appropriate hashtag:

By adding #oscars, it's clear you are talking about the awards ceremony, and not something else. Moreover, if any follower clicks the #oscars link, they'll see all of the other tweets tagged "#oscars".

Sometimes people create funny hashtags. The television host Jimmy Fallon and his writing team are especially skilled at this. They ask their viewing audience a funny question and then tell them to use a hashtag to let the writing team (and other viewers) see the answers. Here's are some of the responses to his hashtag #WorstCarlEverHad:

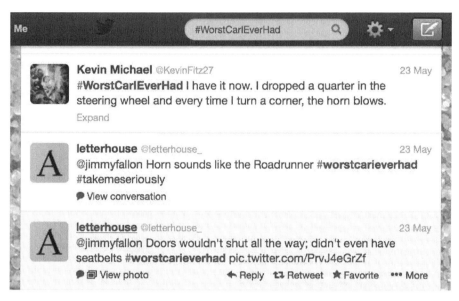

Hashtags are also used to tag sporting events (for instance, #olympics), political races (#election2016), conferences (#ces2014), and practically any other event you can think of.

Hashtag No-Nos

Some new Twitter users make the mistake of turning every word in their tweets into hashtags. Here's an example:

It's irritating and unnecessary. They tweets are hard to read. In addition, hashtagging common nouns, verbs and other words doesn't add any value if people click on the hashtags.

Another mistake involves using the wrong hashtag. For instance, followers of the Boston Red Sox generally use #redsox to talk about their team, not #bostonredsox or #sox.

Mistakes can also happen when a single hashtag is used by two different groups of people. Check out #gastro, which is used by people who like gourmet food as well as doctors and scientists who are interested in discussing gastrointestinal diseases:

Emma Justice @EmmaJustice   16 Mar
Can't decide which of my nine course dinner was the best!
@raymond_blanc @lemanoir #**gastro** dilemma - the canapés?
pic.twitter.com/dNikquQTW7
📷 View photo

victoricko tjhen @victoryTHE   16 Mar
try something different ! #mocktail #**gastro** #punch #fresh #fruits
#photodaily #pictoftheday... instagr.am/p/W7OcvmmXF-/
Expand

2 Minute Medicine @2minmed   16 Mar
#JAMA study finds overuse of #colonoscopy is widespread in the US
| #Medicare #healthcare #**gastro** goo.gl/RrDWe
Expand

Bottom line: Choose your hashtags carefully. If I am interested in using a particular hashtag in a tweet, I often search Twitter first to make sure it's the appropriate one to use.

How Do I Block Someone?

If someone starts following you and you don't want them to, you can block them. To do this, go to your Twitter profile and click the link that shows your followers. Each one will be listed. Next to the Follow/Unfollow button is a drop-down menu that looks like a silhouette. Click it, and select Block.

How Do I Protect My Tweets?

If you don't want your tweets to be seen by the world, or you want more control over who follows you, you can use a Twitter feature called Protect My Tweets. It basically locks down the account so no one except your followers can see what you are tweeting.

To protect your tweets, go to twitter.com and log on. Click the gear icon and select Settings. Then select the menu titled Security And Privacy. Under Privacy, select the Protect My Tweets option:

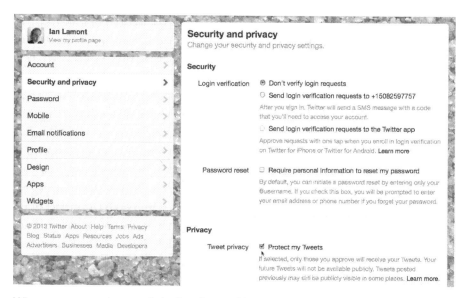

When you are done, click the Save Change button at the bottom of the page.

CHAPTER FOUR

Tweeting

You've created an account, and followed a few people. Now it's time to start tweeting! This chapter explains how to send tweets, participate in discussions and start discussions of your own.

How To Create A Tweet

Creating a new tweet is a cinch. Go to Twitter.com, make sure you are logged in and look for the Compose New tweet field on the left side of the page:

Place your cursor in the field, and start typing. As you type, a counter below the field counts down how many characters you have left. Once you have typed 140 characters, the number will turn negative, meaning it will be truncated unless you cut it down to size. When you are ready to release your tweet to the world, click the Tweet button.

Twitter's mobile apps are also easy to use, although they will require you to use a smaller keyboard. Look for the Compose icon, which looks like a note with a pen atop it. Then use the keyboard or the dictation function on your device to create the tweet. Here is the iPad view:

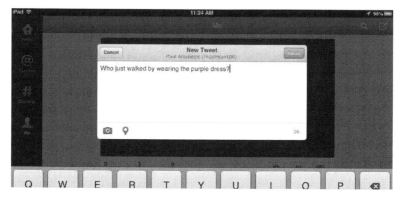

Tap the Tweet button when you are ready to send it.

What Should I Say On Twitter?

While creating a tweet is easy, deciding what to tweet about can be tricky for newcomers. Keep in mind that writing great tweets will involve understanding your audience, and seeing what works for them. Sometimes it's helpful to look to other people for inspiration, but as I explain in this section, the tone of the conversation can change depending on who you follow. I also discuss how to get past mental blocks associated with using this new medium for the first time. Finally, I have some practical tips about how to come up with great tweets to get the ball rolling.

What Do Other People Usually Tweet About?

What kinds of things do people tweet about in their 140-character messages? It really depends on who you follow. In Chapter 1, I showed you some individual examples of tweets by a famous person (@Oprah), a small business (@Momogoose) and several ordinary users. But if you follow hundreds of people, chances are you will see some patterns emerge, based on their interests.

For instance, if I were to use a phrase to describe the tweets from the 400-odd people I follow (a mix of journalists, tech/Web people, people from the

Boston area and random friends), it would be "observations and questions about life and careers, with some overlap, especially when major events take place."

Here's another way to break it down:

Observations and questions: People have interests, activities, and professional backgrounds, which will be reflected in their tweets. Someone has just finished a book, cooked a meal, taken a jog or commented on the weather. Occasionally, people will ask questions.

Overlap: At any given time, a few accounts out of the 400 appear to be watching the same TV show or sporting event. On Friday night, some of the younger people will tweet from a club or bar. Because I follow so many technology people, I see a lot of references to companies such as Google, Apple, and Microsoft.

Major events: When there's a major event, such as a natural disaster, political scandal or a major gadget release, there is a surge of topical tweets as the people I follow react to or "retweet" the news (more about retweeting later in this chapter). For instance, the night Steve Jobs died, about half of the people I followed had something to say about it. National elections also bring out a lot of Twitter commentary.

But here's the thing: What I see is not representative of what other people see. A fashionista in Manhattan will have a far different experience with Twitter, based on her interests and the people she follows. She will see more tweets and photos involving clothing, shoes, accessories, and sales, as well as more information specific to New York City.

The football fan in Florida is more likely to follow other football fans, and their tweets are more likely to include football references. A programmer who lives in Paris is more likely to see tweets about programming and his or her neighborhood in the 19th arrondissement. What about a housewife in Hollywood? Or a scientist in Singapore? They will follow different types of people, and will see and send different types of tweets.

Of course, you can follow the cue of the people you follow and start tweeting about similar things. But it's also possible to develop your own voice, as I describe below.

Mental Blocks To Tweeting

A lot of people feel strange using Twitter for the first time. "Why would anyone care about what I have to say?" is one comment I hear from new users. Others feel slightly uncomfortable sharing information publicly, even if the information is not particularly sensitive or important. A few people complain they don't have enough room to say what they want to say in just 140 characters.

Here are some responses to put your mind at ease:

"The stuff I have to say is too boring." Yes, most people won't be particularly interested in the fact that your cat Mr. Elmer P. McFurrikins is curled up on the couch right now, and boy, doesn't he look cute?

But tweets about the mundane aspects of your life contain something that is vitally important to gaining followers and taking part in discussions: *Authenticity*. tweets about the weather, the crowds at the mall, your kid's basketball game and even your cat demonstrate that you are a real person, are probably friendly, and are willing to share information about your life. Some people may even want to start a discussion about these topics. Considering the number of cat people in the world, I wouldn't be surprised if you got a response like this:

"I'm uncomfortable sharing information publicly." The idea of posting opinions, observations and other snippets of life for others (including complete strangers) to see can be a little unnerving at first. For some people, it's an unfamiliar concept. For others, there is a worry about tweeting something that might put them in a bad light. And then there are those who like the idea of tweeting, but get concerned that certain people might spot a specific tweet ("What will my boss/neighbor/ex-boyfriend think if they see the tweet I made on Saturday?").

With Twitter, keep in mind that *you don't have to share any more information than you want to share*. Here are tips for dialing things down to keep them at a level that makes you comfortable:

- You don't have to use a real name in your Twitter handle when you create your account. If @bobcsmith22 is too revealing, use @bobbiec22 or @turtleman4.

- You can remove elements from your Twitter profile, or substitute more anonymous information. You don't have to use a real name. You can leave your location and profile picture blank.

- Don't use the names of your family members or friends.

- If you are about to tweet something that might be considered controversial or offensive, take some time to think about it before posting.

On this last point, you can also use softer language. For instance, after seeing dog doo in the local park, you might be inclined to fire off an angry tweet:

That's liable to rub all dog owners the wrong way. How about tweeting this, which not only clarifies who is at fault, but also starts a dialogue?

One final comment regarding controversial tweets: Check your employer's social media or online communications policies before tweeting about work-related issues.

"140 characters isn't enough to say what I want to say!" I used to be like this. As a blogger used to writing hundreds of words at a time, the idea of short bursts on Twitter seemed so...limiting. But I quickly learned you can actually say quite a bit with 140 characters. Observations can be brief, identifying the key pieces of information:

Opinions don't have to be long, either, as in this tweet about a San Francisco/Seattle football game:

And when deep analysis or description is required, that's when posting photographs and links to long-form material comes in handy.

Lastly, Twitter teaches you to be spare with words. The character counter can inform you if a tweet is too long:

The tweet, which is twice as long as Twitter allows, was eventually reduced to:

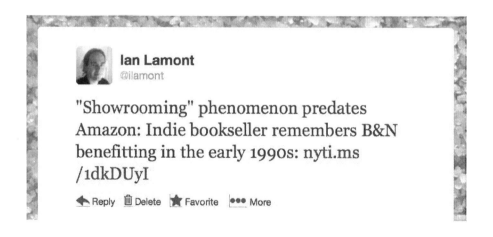

Tips For Writing Great Tweets

So you've gotten over your hang-ups about tweeting. Now here's where the rubber hits the road. It's time to start tweeting! But what can you tweet about?

The obvious answer is "anything you feel comfortable sharing," but I'm going to make it a little easier for you by suggesting a few ways to get those creative juices flowing.

Tip #1: What did you see/hear/experience in the last 24 hours that was notable?

It could have been a memorable play in last night's football game, the Chinese food you ate for lunch, the classic song you're listening to now, or a change in the weather:

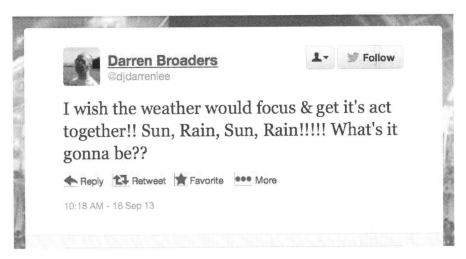

Tip #2: Take A Picture!

When you write a tweet on Twitter.com (left) or using the Twitter mobile app (right), you'll notice a camera icon that appears below the text field:

Clicking or tapping the camera allows you to choose a photo to include in your tweet. The photo may already exist on your hard drive or mobile phone, or you can create a new one (if you are using a phone or tablet). Twitter will upload the photo to its servers, and then will create a short link that will be added to the tweet. Anyone clicking on the link will be able to see the picture (or will be displayed automatically).

As you might expect, people like to share photos of interesting or beautiful sights, as well as food, pets and family vacations. But I've also seen people using photos to illustrate a situation, such as a car with an unusual license plate:

(Note: Never take a picture or attempt to tweet while you are driving)

One of the most interesting photos I've seen recently: A photo from an airplane of fuel being jettisoned before an aborted transpacific flight:

The plane landed safely. The person who took that photo wasn't the only passenger on that flight to share his experience or the frustration associated with waiting to be rebooked.

What photos should you share on Twitter? It depends on what you think is interesting…or what you think your audience will like. Try a few shots, and see how people react!

Tip #3: What made you laugh out loud?

Humor is all around you. Colleagues, neighbors, children and strangers will sometimes say or do something that makes you laugh. TV shows and other mass media are another source of laughter. These moments can be shared on Twitter. And, of course, one liners are made for Twitter:

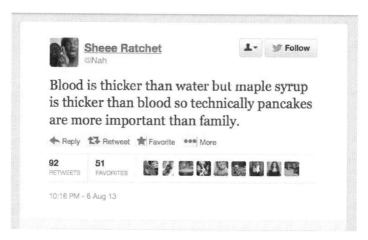

Tip #4: What tidbit would you share with your neighbors?

Neighbors could be the people who live near you, or fellow cube-dwellers congregating at the water cooler. What sorts of tidbits that you might share with them could also be shared publicly? Certainly not malicious gossip, personal details or information that's not meant to be shared ("Did you see how plastered Dave got at the barbecue?"). But other bits of neighborly news that you or other people might say aloud can be shared on Twitter:

Tip #5: What would you say on Facebook?

In many cases, information or observations you share on Facebook can be pasted directly into Twitter afterward. There are even Twitter applications that allow people to post to Facebook and Twitter simultaneously, without copying and pasting. On the official companion website for *Twitter In 30 Minutes* (twitter.in30minutes.com) I have included a review of one such application called Hootsuite.

Of course, do not tweet information that's meant to stay in a closed conversation on Facebook. Remember, on Twitter, almost all tweets are public.

Tip #6: Share an interesting link

Sharing links on Twitter is a great way to spread news, videos, shopping deals or useful online resources. It's easy to do, and Twitter automatically substitutes a shortened link to make sure you don't go over the 140-character limit.

The easy way to share a link:

You may notice that many articles, blogs, YouTube videos and websites have icons, buttons, or links that say "Tweet" or show the Twitter icon:

If you click the button or link, it will allow you to share the headline and the link on Twitter. Regardless of whether you are on a desktop computer or smartphone, you may be prompted to log into Twitter to allow sharing the link with your followers. Unless you have a reason to suspect that the website is malicious, it's OK to do this.

You may also be able to edit the tweet before it goes out, but don't edit or delete the link, which is required in order to let your followers view the webpage. Press "Submit", and the link will be shared.

The hard way to share a link:

You will need two browsers open at the same time, or two browser tabs.

- Open up one browser with Twitter. The other browser should have the news story, video or Web page displayed, along with the URL in the address bar.

- Copy the headline (right-click with your mouse, or select Edit>Copy).

- Switch to the browser with Twitter, and paste the headline into the area where you compose a tweet (right-click, or select Edit>Paste). Or type a summary or your opinion ("Must-read article about the Flying Burrito Brothers").

- Go back to the browser window with the interesting webpage. Go to the address bar and copy the entire URL.

- Switch to the browser with Twitter, and paste the URL after the headline or text you've written.

- Make sure there is a space between the text and the headline in your tweet.

- Don't worry if the tweet is too long — Twitter will substitute a short link.

- Press the Send button

Tip #7: Ask other people for help

Twitter is a great place to ask for advice. I'm not talking about serious, soul-searching questions ("Should I marry him?", "What did Lennon mean by 'Strawberry Fields Forever'?", "How should I tell my boss his VP of sales is getting kickbacks?) but rather the quick questions that your followers or other Twitter denizens may be able to help with. For instance:

I've found that adding a hashtagged topic can help generate responses. For instance, if I were asking about the best Cuban restaurant in Miami, adding #Miami to the end of the tweet will generate some additional eyeballs from people who follow that topic, but don't follow you.

How To Delete Tweets

So you've created a tweet. What if you want to get rid of it?

On the Web:

1. Go to Twitter.com and click on your name, or on the link that shows the total number of tweets you've made. This will bring up a reverse-chronological list of all of your tweets.

2. Hover your mouse over the tweet you want to delete. Some small icons and links will appear, including one labeled "Delete". Click it.

3. You will be asked, "Are you sure you want to delete?" Confirm your selection.

The tweet is gone!

Phone or tablet:

1. Open your Twitter application

2. Tap the Profile icon, which will show a list of your recent tweets (select View All tweets to see older tweets).

3. Tap the tweet you want to delete.

4. Tap the trash can icon.

5. You will be asked to confirm whether you want to delete it. Select "Yes".

The tweet will be removed from your stream.

Regardless of which method you use to delete a specific tweet, it may still live on if someone else has retweeted it or it's been manually saved by other people.

CHAPTER FIVE

Advanced Twitter: Joining The Discussion

Twitter is not just about one-way tweets. It's possible to connect, share, and discuss using a variety of methods. Some of these conventions may seem weird, or employ unfamiliar syntax, such as the letters "RT" and lots of "@" symbols and hashtags. Once you understand how the syntax works, you'll realize Twitter discussions in many ways mirror the ways humans have always talked and shared information.

However, the scale of the service, and the ability of a single tweet to reach thousands or even millions of people in a short period of time can create an amplification effect that is seldom seen in other mediums.

Read on to learn how to carry a conversation forward on Twitter.

Someone Responded To My Tweet! What Do I Do?

One day, you may receive a notification that looks like this:

People can create a so-called "@reply" (pronounced "at-reply") by clicking the reply link below a tweet. Try it on any tweet in your feed. You'll see that Twitter automatically starts the reply with the Twitter handle of the person you are responding to. Then it's up to you to type in additional text, which might be a comment or additional piece of information.

Note that @replies won't be seen by other users unless they too follow the account that starts the tweet, or are actively looking at all of the tweets from a specific account. So, if by some miracle @Oprah sent an @reply to one of your tweets, none of your followers will see it, unless they are also following @Oprah.

You can see a list of all interactions involving your Twitter account (including @replies) by clicking or tapping the Connect menu (look for the "@" symbol at the top of the screen). You will then see a list of interactions, including @replies, @mentions and retweets (explained below), and tweets that have been favorited by other people:

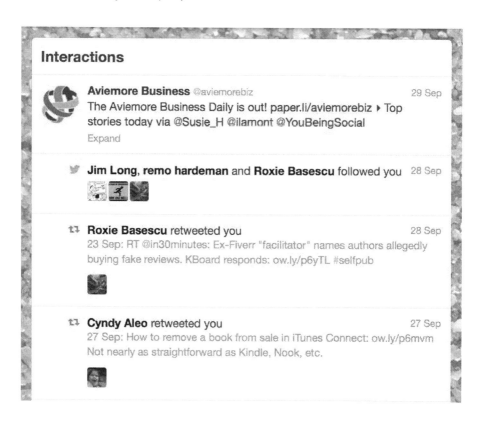

Someone Mentioned Me!

When browsing the Connect screen, you may notice tweets from other people that contain your Twitter handle, but are not responding to a question. Here's an example:

These are called @mentions (pronounced "at-mentions"). They are often acknowledgements of a piece of information, or a question that is directed at you. Sometimes they are intended to draw your attention to something. For instance, every day scores of people @mention the Twitter handle of a Boston-based blog called Universal Hub, to draw the editor's attention to some piece of local news:

If you receive an @mention, it's up to you how to respond. In many cases, no response is necessary.

Unfortunately, spammers and malicious hackers have latched onto @mentions. They know that you will probably read a tweet that includes your Twitter handle, and use @mentions to spread links to porn, coupon sites and sites that install malware on visitors' computers. Be suspicious of short click-bait that mentions your Twitter handle and includes a link to an unfamiliar website. If it's from an unfamiliar Twitter account with a small number of previous tweets, it's probably spam.

Retweets

Retweet, v. to repeat someone else's tweet, while giving credit to the original author; n. A tweet that has been copied and rebroadcast on another Twitter account, with the capital letters "RT" and the Twitter handle of the original sender added to the front of the new tweet.

You've just read my definition of a retweet, but an example should make the concept clear:

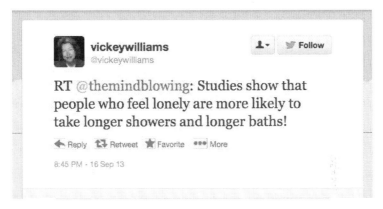

What's going on here? @themindblowing originally tweeted a summary of the behavioral studies. @vickeywilliams liked what she saw, or otherwise thought it was noteworthy, and decided to say it again. She did not type out the whole tweet by hand. She hovered over the Retweet link below the message, which automatically copies the handle of the author and the content of the original tweet, and then sends it from @vickeywilliams.

Notice that @vickeywilliams acknowledged the original author by including @themindblowing's Twitter handle. If she had simply copied the message, but not credited the source, that's not a retweet — that's just copying.

Why do people retweet other people's tweets? Often, it's for the same reason that people might repeat what they heard from a friend, coworker or neighbor — it's information, news or a clever phrase that's worth repeating.

Some people, when RTing someone else, like to add a little comment before the RT symbol ("Agreed!" or "Read this"). Others may shorten the original to ensure the extra characters don't push the retweet over 140 characters.

Going Viral

Twitter discussions and retweets can sometimes lead to a piece of news, a photo or some other information "going viral." Here's what it looks like:

As you can see, eight other Twitter accounts retweeted this piece of information. What happens then are some followers of those eight retweet it again, then each of the retweets are again retweeted by *their* followers, and so on...kind of like the old shampoo commercial!

If it gets retweeted enough, what often happens is some celebrity, politician, major news organization or some other widely followed or trusted source will retweet it, at which point hundreds of thousands or even millions of people are retweeting the same piece of information in a short period of time.

When something goes viral, it can lead to more followers and publicity for the person who first tweeted the information.

But there is a dark side to going viral, too. What if the information is wrong?

This is not hypothetical situation. It's happened before. Someone tweets incorrect information, it snowballs, and later it turns out that the information was false. In extreme cases, people have had their deaths prematurely reported, or have been fingered for crimes they did not commit. By the time the truth comes out, reputations have been damaged or long explanations are in order.

Because of the potential for false information to spread virally through retweets, I advise people to be careful when retweeting details relating to crimes, disasters or scandals. Innocent people can be hurt when false rumors are retweeted. Check the news or some other reliable source first.

Advanced Features

While we don't have enough time to cover all aspects of Twitter, there are a few additional features and tools you should be aware of. They include Direct Messages, Favorites, Lists, and Shortcut Keys.

Direct Messages

Direct Messages are kind of like text messages. This feature lets you send a 140-character message directly to another person. However, the sender and the recipient must be following each other on Twitter. To see or send a direct message, go to your profile page and click the icon that looks like an envelope.

Favorites

If you follow a lot of people, you may want to mark interesting or special tweets created by others. If you hover over the tweet with your mouse, you will see the Favorite link. Clicking it adds the tweet to your list of favorites, which you can review later.

Lists

Lists are a way of organizing Twitter accounts. Here are some examples:

- A list of people in your hometown with Twitter accounts.
- People you work with.
- Famous bands who are on Twitter.
- Thought leaders in the real estate industry.
- Comedians on Twitter.

Viewing a list's timeline displays the recent tweets from the people on the list. To see the lists that you've created or you have been assigned to, go to twitter.com, open your profile, and click on the Lists link in the left column.

You can create a new list and add an account to it by opening a profile page and clicking on the symbol that looks like a silhouette. Then, select "Add or remove from lists":

You do not need to follow an account to add them to a list. Note also that lists can be seen by other people. In other words, if you create a list of Twitter accounts with funny profile pictures, not only will other people be able to see it, but the people you have added to the list will know about it, too.

Shortcut Keys

On twitter.com, there is an easy way to perform most common functions, such as creating a new tweet, replying, searching, or scrolling down. All you need to do is press one of the following letters or symbols on the keyboard to activate the following functions:

- **N** – Create a new tweet.
- **J** – Select the first tweet in the timeline. Subsequent presses select the next tweet in line.
- **K** – Select the previous tweet.

- **T** – Retweet selected tweet.
- **R** – Reply to selected tweet.
- **Space bar** – Scroll down. This is a great way to rapidly view recent tweets in your timeline.
- **Forward slash** – Places the cursor in search field.

There are about a dozen more shortcut keys for more obscure or advanced functions. If you are on twitter.com, press the shift and question mark keys at the same time to see them all.

CHAPTER SIX
Conclusion

In 30 minutes, you've learned the basics of Twitter, from creating an account to taking part in discussions. You now have a foundation of knowledge and practical skills which you can use to make new connections, share information and better understand the world around you.

While it feels good knowing how Twitter works and what you can do with it, to really get value from Twitter, you have to regularly use it. After setting up your account, you should follow a few dozen interesting accounts, using the advice I gave in Chapter 3 or via the list of cool Twitter accounts to follow on the official book website (twitter.in30minutes.com):

Then start tweeting. You don't have to be fanatical, but try doing at least two tweets per day. It will help you get comfortable with Twitter, and develop your own unique "voice." Regular tweeting also will help you attract followers and engage in discussions. Be sure to ask questions if you need help — people on Twitter generally like to help new users. Make an effort to retweet other people's interesting tweets. If you see an opportunity to help someone out on Twitter, do it. It can be as simple as answering a question or showing support in some other way.

Be sure to visit the official companion website at twitter.in30minutes.com to get more tips. There is a series of videos that show you how to perform basic actions (deleting tweets, retweeting something, etc.) as well as posts that deal with advanced features. You also can find reviews of special applications that extend the functionality of Twitter, such as Hootsuite. The book website also contains links to other In 30 Minutes® guides, including *LinkedIn In 30 Minutes* by author Melanie Pinola and *Online Content Marketing In 30 Minutes*, by Derek Slater.

In you're interested in connecting with me, I've listed my contact details and other information in a personal message on the next page.

Thanks for purchasing *Twitter In 30 Minutes*, and I hope to see you soon on Twitter!

A Message From The Author, And A Request

Writing *Twitter In 30 Minutes* was a labor of love. I have been an enthusiastic user of Twitter for more than five years. During this time, I have used Twitter to connect with people, discover information, and share photos, quips and random observations about the world. Twitter has introduced me to new friends and experiences that I otherwise would never have had. I am happy to share what I have learned with my readers, and I hope your own Twitter journey is similarly rewarding. If you have a question about Twitter or the guide, please feel free to email me at ian@in30minutes.com.

I would also like to ask a favor. Could you take a minute to rate *Twitter In 30 Minutes* and write a quick review? You can do so on these sites:

- **Amazon.com**
- **BarnesAndNoble.com**
- **Goodreads.com**

An honest appraisal of the contents of *Twitter In 30 Minutes* will not only be appreciated by me, but it will also let other potential readers know what to expect.

Lastly, I welcome any reader to follow me on Twitter. My handle is @ilamont. If you follow me and use an @mention on Twitter to let me know that you own the guide, you will get a special Twitter shout-out and I will follow you back.

Thanks for reading!

Ian Lamont

P.S.: If you are interested in browsing other *In 30 Minutes* guides, please visit in30minutes.com to see the available titles. To be notified of future releases, you can sign up for our free e-newsletter at in30minutes.com/newsletter, or like our Facebook page at facebook.com/in30minutes.

About The Author

Ian Lamont is a former technology and business journalist whose writing and editorial work have garnered numerous awards. He has authored several In 30 Minutes® guides, including *Twitter In 30 Minutes*, *Dropbox In 30 Minutes*, *Google Drive & Docs In 30 Minutes*, and *Excel Basics In 30 Minutes*.

His media career has spanned more than 20 years across three continents, including a stint in the British music business and a six-year residence in Taipei, where he learned Mandarin and worked for a local TV network and newspaper.

It was while living overseas that Lamont encountered the World Wide Web for the first time. He was immediately inspired by the power of this new platform. After learning HTML and other Web technologies, he built websites for Harvard University and developed new online services for technology publisher IDG. He was the senior editor, new media for IDG's *Computerworld* and served as the managing editor of *The Industry Standard*. Later, Lamont founded two start-up ventures, including a mobile software company and i30 Media Corporation, which publishes In 30 Minutes® guides.

Lamont is a graduate of the Boston University College of Communication, the Harvard Extension School, and MIT's Sloan Fellows Program in Innovation and Global Leadership. He lives in the Boston area. When he's not working or writing, he likes to spend time with his family, conduct genealogical research and improve his Chinese cooking skills.

Credits

All photos and screenshots were taken by the author. The cover design was created by Steve Sauer of Single Fin Design. Monica Hamilton was the copy editor.

Bonus: Introduction To *Dropbox In 30 Minutes*

(The following chapter is the introduction to Dropbox In 30 Minutes, *by Ian Lamont. It is available through Amazon, iTunes, Barnes & Noble, and other marketplaces via dropbox.in30minutes.com)*

Got 30 minutes to spare? Good — it's all you'll need to master the basics of Dropbox.

Dropbox is an easy way to store and share photos, documents, spreadsheets, and other types of computer files. Much like the introduction of email, digital photography, and low-rise athletic socks, once you get the hang of Dropbox, you'll wonder how you ever got along without it.

Dropbox works by keeping an identical copy of selected files on your computer(s) and Dropbox's cloud-based storage system, and *automatically synchronizing* them over an encrypted Internet connection. I've put asterisks around "automatically synchronizing," because this is the killer feature of Dropbox, something that will save lots of time and streamline collaboration. It's cited repeatedly in this guide.

What does Dropbox's automatic syncing feature enable? Here are some common scenarios:

- Mark uses Dropbox to **share a folder full of documents with four coworkers**, so they can work on spreadsheets and other documents together.

- Jennifer **backs up the photos that she takes on her iPhone**, without using cables. She can immediately access the photos on her laptop.

- Chris **instantly backs up the files he's working on** in Dropbox. If his computer crashes, he can easily recover them.

Besides *automatic syncing*, another advantage of Dropbox is it follows the same conventions that people already use to save files, create folders, and move stuff around on their computers. This means your Dropbox data will always appear in the familiar "My Computer" (Windows) or Finder (Mac) windows on your computer. As a result, Dropbox is very easy to learn.

But is Dropbox right for you? Ask yourself if any of the following statements apply to your own technology practices:

- You back up files by **emailing them to yourself**.
- You transfer files between two computers **using a USB drive**.
- You want a **better way** to store and manage digital photos.
- You need to **collaborate** on documents and **share files** with coworkers.
- You're a **total klutz** who is apt to lose all of the important data on your laptop by **dropping it into the swimming pool**.

If you found yourself nodding as you read this list, then Dropbox will be an extremely useful utility and time-saver.

Dropbox is also a free service, although heavy users will opt to buy more storage space. But there are several official ways (as well as a few tricks) to get more free storage space, as explained in Chapter 5, "Dropbox — The Rogue FAQ." You'll find many other useful time-saving tips and ways to use Dropbox throughout the brief.

Before we get going, it's good to have a computer handy, or a smartphone, or a tablet. This way, you can quickly try out some the things discussed in this guide. Or you can just read through all of the chapters and install Dropbox later.

Let's get started with Dropbox!

To read the rest of this book, visit dropbox.in30minutes.com.

Bonus: Introduction To *LinkedIn In 30 Minutes*

(The following bonus chapter is the introduction to LinkedIn In 30 Minutes, *by author Melanie Pinola. To download the ebook or purchase the paperback, visit the book's official website, linkedin.in30minutes.com)*

If you're serious about taking your career to the next level, you need to be on LinkedIn. In the past five years, the online career network has opened doors for millions of people, transforming the way they market themselves and enabling them to vastly expand their professional networks. In addition, companies are using LinkedIn to recruit everyone from entry-level employees to CEOs. In the next 30 minutes, this guide will show you how to best present yourself on LinkedIn and leverage other features that will help advance your career.

LinkedIn is the world's largest professional network, with more than 200 million members and counting. Hiring managers and headhunters actively use LinkedIn. Companies big and small, and millions of professionals — including executives from every Fortune 500 company — use it. You need to actively use it, too. The reason is simple: **There's no better social networking tool (or other online tool, for that matter) for furthering your career than LinkedIn.**

That's a bold statement, but research backs it up. Consider this:

- 98% of recruiters used social media to find talent in 2012, according to a Bullhorn survey. Guess which network they used to place job candidates? That's right — LinkedIn. Some 93% of the surveyed staffing professionals placed candidates through LinkedIn, compared to just 17% for Facebook and 13% for Twitter.
- Another Bullhorn survey of over 77,500 recruiters found that 48% of them post jobs on LinkedIn *and nowhere else on social media*.
- 90% of surveyed LinkedIn users said they thought the site is useful because:
    - "It helps me to connect to individuals in my industry as possible clients"

- "It is more professional than Facebook"
- "It allows me to hire people that I wouldn't regularly meet"

Although many people think of LinkedIn mostly as a tool for job seekers, you can benefit substantially from using LinkedIn even if you're not ready to leave your current job. **Think of the site as a free online résumé, industry insights tool, and digital Rolodex rolled into one.**

Here are a few ways people are using LinkedIn to achieve their career goals:

- **Dan is an IT professional who's satisfied with his current job** … but he wouldn't say "no" if a more attractive opportunity presented itself! He doesn't actively check job boards, but he set up his LinkedIn profile so headhunters can easily find him.

- **Gabe is the owner of a small accounting firm**. He uses LinkedIn to promote his services to potential and current clients, discuss business strategies and general accounting topics with other LinkedIn members, and keep up with his competitors' developments.

- **Dana is a recent college graduate** who just got her first job doing graphic design. She uses LinkedIn to share — and discover — interesting information about her field, help her grow her expertise and build her professional reputation.

- **Mike has been out of work for over a year**, after huge layoffs at the manufacturing company where he used to work. LinkedIn helps him update and modernize his résumé, find companies currently hiring for his skills set, and connect with previous colleagues, employers, and classmates who could help him re-enter the workforce.

- **Jonathan is a mid-level marketing manager** who's been at the same company for the last 10 years with little advancement — and he's ready to move up! He uses LinkedIn to find relevant job openings, research and follow companies he's interested in, and find people in his network who could help with his job search.

While these people are in different stages of their careers and use LinkedIn for different purposes, they have two things in common: They're interested in maintaining or advancing their careers, and LinkedIn is central to their career development strategies. Facebook might be great for socializing and Twitter for keeping abreast of the news (or following celebrities), but LinkedIn is for your livelihood.

Note also that even though LinkedIn once targeted people working in technology-related industries and white-collar professionals, the network has since expanded to every occupation and industry. You can be a chef, a cardiologist, or a carpenter, yet still build a network and find other ways to leverage LinkedIn.

Whether you're completely new to LinkedIn or have already set up an account but are left thinking "What now?", this guide is for you. In just 30 minutes, you'll learn the basics of getting started with LinkedIn, such as how to:

- Create a strong LinkedIn profile (Chapter 1)
- Build and grow your professional network (Chapter 2)
- Use LinkedIn to find a job, stay current in your industry, and advance your career (Chapters 3 and 4)
- Make even better use of LinkedIn with power user tricks such as organizing your LinkedIn contacts and changing privacy settings (Chapter 5, and online at linkedin.in30minutes.com)

At the end of each chapter is a convenient checklist, which will help ensure that you have hit the most important steps.

By the way, if you're the type of person who cringes when someone gushes about "networking," don't worry. As a shy, card-carrying introvert, "networking" is not my favorite word either. One of the great things about LinkedIn is this isn't the same kind of networking that happens at conventions, where you're wearing a name tag, trying to meet strangers, and awkwardly attempting to make small talk. **LinkedIn is networking without the pressure**. Using the service, you can reach out to people you know — and those they know — virtually. In fact, people expect to be contacted, and others might also reach out to you. That's what the site is for!

Ready to get started? Now's a great time to find a copy of your most recently updated résumé and fire up your browser...

To learn more about LinkedIn In 30 Minutes, or to purchase the ebook or paperback edition, please visit linkedin.in30minutes.com.

Bonus: Introduction To *Excel Basics In 30 Minutes*

(The following chapter is from Excel Basics In 30 Minutes, *by Ian Lamont. If you're interested in buying a copy, visit the official book website at excel.in30minutes.com)*

Some years ago, a colleague came over to my cubicle and asked for some help. John wanted to create a long list of names, categorize them, and assign a score on a scale of one to 10 for each one. Then, he wanted to do things with the list, such as identifying the top scores and creating category averages.

John knew I was familiar with all kinds of desktop and online software. He asked, "Which one would you recommend for this type of task?"

"That's easy," I answered. "Enter the data into Microsoft Excel or Google Spreadsheets. You can then alphabetize the list, sort by the highest and lowest scores, and draw out category averages. You can even create neat-looking charts based on the results." I used Excel to whip up a basic list, and emailed him the file.

John thanked me profusely, but admitted, "I have only the vaguest idea about and almost no experience with spreadsheets."

John's situation is not unusual. Millions of people know that Excel can be used for tracking financial data and number crunching. They may have even opened Excel and entered some numbers into a corporate expense worksheet.

Nevertheless, Excel suffers from an image problem. Most people assume that spreadsheet programs such as Excel are intended for accountants, analysts, financiers, scientists, mathematicians, and other geeky types. Creating a spreadsheet, sorting data, using functions, and making charts seems daunting, and best left to the nerds.

I'm here to tell you that spreadsheets are not just for nerds. Practically anyone can use Excel for work, school, personal projects and other uses. I've written this guide to help you quickly get up to speed on basic concepts, using plain English, step-by-step instructions, and lots of screenshots. Thirty minutes from now, you'll know how to:

- Create a spreadsheet and enter numbers and text into cells.
- Perform addition, multiplication, and other simple mathematical functions.
- Derive values based on percentages.
- Perform time-saving tasks, such as sorting large lists and automatically applying the same formula across a range of values.
- Make great-looking charts.

You can imagine how these techniques can help in real-world situations, from tracking household expenses to making sales projections. You can even use them to organize events, and track the office football pool.

We only have 30 minutes, so let's get started!

To read more of Excel Basics In 30 Minutes *and download free sample spreadsheets and videos, visit excel.in30minutes.com.*

Bonus: Introduction To

Google Drive & Docs In 30 Minutes

(The following bonus chapter is the introduction to Google Drive & Docs In 30 Minutes, *by author Ian Lamont. If you're interested in downloading the ebook or purchasing the paperback, please visit the guide's official website, googledrive.in30minutes.com.)*

Thanks for your interest in *Google Drive & Docs In 30 Minutes*. I wrote this unofficial user guide to help people get up to speed with Google Drive, a remarkable (and free) online office suite that includes a word processor (Docs), spreadsheet program (Sheets), and slideshow tool (Slides). The guide also covers the storage features of Google Drive.

How do people use Google Drive and Docs? There are many possible uses. Consider these examples:

- **A harried product manager needs to continue work on an important proposal over the weekend**. In the past, she would have dug around in her purse to look for an old USB drive she uses for transferring files. Or, she might have emailed herself an attachment to open at home. Instead, she saves the Word document and an Excel spreadsheet to Google Drive at the office. Later that evening, on her home PC, she opens her Google Drive folder to access the Excel file. All of her saves are updated to Google Drive. When she returns to work the following Monday, the updated data can be viewed on her workstation.

- **The organizer of a family reunion wants to survey 34 cousins about attendance, lodging preferences, and potluck dinner preparation** (always a challenge — the Nebraska branch of the family won't eat corn or Garbanzo beans). He emails everyone a link to a Web Form created in Google Drive. The answers are automatically transferred to Google Sheets, where he can see the responses and tally the results.

- **A small business consultant is helping the owner of Slappy's**

Canadian Diner ("We Put The Canadian Back In Bacon") prepare a slideshow for potential franchisees in Ohio. The consultant and Slappy collaborate using Google Slides, which lets them remotely access the deck and add text, images, and other elements. The consultant shares a link to the slideshow with her consulting partner, so he can periodically review it on a Web browser and check for problems. Later, Slappy meets his potential franchise operators at a hotel in Cleveland, and uses Slides to give them his pitch.

- **An elementary school faculty uses Google Docs to collaborate on lesson plans**. Each teacher accesses the same document from their homes or classrooms. Updates are instantly reflected, even when two teachers are simultaneously accessing the same document. Their principal (known as "Skinner" behind his back) is impressed by how quickly the faculty completes the plans, and how well the curriculums are integrated.

- **At the same school, the 5th-grade teachers ask their students to submit homework using Docs**. The teachers add corrections and notes, which the students can access at any time via a Web browser. It's much more efficient than emailing attachments around, and the students don't need to bug their parents to buy expensive word-processing programs.

Many people try Google Docs because it's free (Google Drive is, too, if you store less than five gigabytes of data). Microsoft Office can cost hundreds of dollars, and the programs in Apple's iWork suite cost nearly $60. While Google Docs is not as sophisticated, it handles the basics very well. Docs also offers a slew of powerful online features that are unmatched by Office or iWork, including:

- The ability to review the history of a specific document, and revert to an earlier version.

- Simple Web forms and online surveys that can be produced without programming skills or website hosting arrangements.

- Collaboration features that let users work on the same document in real time.

- Offline file storage that can be synced to multiple computers.

- Automatic notification of the release date of Brad Pitt's next movie.

I'm just kidding about the last item. But Google Drive and Docs really can do those other things, and without the help of your company's IT department or the pimply teenager from down the street. These features are built right into the software, and are ready to use as soon as you've signed up.

Even though the myriad features of Google Drive may seem overwhelming, this guide makes it easy to get started. *Google Drive & Docs In 30 Minutes* is written in plain English, with lots of step-by-step instructions, screenshots and tips. Videos and other resources are available on the companion website to this book, googledrive.in30minutes.com. You'll get up to speed in no time.

We've only got a half-hour, so let's get started with Google Drive and Docs!

If you're interested in learning more about this title, or buying the ebook or paperback, visit the official website located at googledrive.in30minutes.com.

More In 30 Minutes® Guides

What do you want to learn in 30 minutes?

Full list of titles at in30minutes.com